THE UK SC
SURVIVAL

WRITE A
SCRIPT
IN

BY TIM CLAGUE
& DANNY STACK

Foreword by Tim John

FOREWORD

By Tim John

As a Hollywood screenwriter who's also spent some time teaching the craft, I know how daunting most people can find the idea of writing a screenplay. That's why I love this guide – because it provides really clear, practical steps to help you get past every writer's worst nightmare (staring at that blank page/computer screen), so you're looking at a complete first draft. And not just any old first draft, but one that incorporates all the elements industry buyers are going to look out for when they consider buying a script.

So, if you're going to invest in your screenwriting career, why not start here?

Tim John
Screenwriter
A Street Cat Named Bob (and a few other things)

TEN WEEKS IN TEN CHAPTERS

ABOUT THIS BOOK

Did you know that in Hollywood you get ten weeks to write the first draft of a script? So why don't we use that timeframe to beat our own procrastination and get a first draft script done, no excuses. The focus and recommendations here will be based on genre ideas (i.e. commercial tastes). If you want to write a TV script, no problem, we'll get into that as well. Whatever the case, if you're up for the writing challenge, then let's get to work.

Included in this book are some individual ideas and thoughts in addition to the main advice. They will appear in these speech marks.

TIM AND DANNY WHO?

We're not big famous writers. We're not academics either. We're a couple of writers and filmmakers who make a living out of what we do. We wrote *The UK Scriptwriter's Survival Handbook*, which focuses on how to make a living as a working writer and is very much a practical guide. The core theme is being proactive and getting on with the work at hand. This new handbook is on that same theme. It's a practical book to help you keep on track.

Tim

Tim Clague wrote the BAFTA-nominated short film *Eight*, the story of a young boy's quest to find out about his dad. Since then he has written and directed an array of short films that have screened at international festivals and won awards. Tim also has broadcast credits with ITV and BBC.

Danny

Danny's TV writing credits include *EastEnders*, *Doctors* and high-profile children's shows including *Octonauts*, *Hey Duggee* and *Thunderbirds Are Go*. For many years he was a story analyst for companies such as Working

Title, Pathé, Miramax and UK Film Council. He also set up the Red Planet Prize, a scheme to discover new writers, with writer/producer Tony Jordan.

Together

Tim and Danny created the UK Scriptwriters podcast in 2010. This led to a further partnership across screenwriting talks/workshops, adverts and corporate films. They took their collaboration a step further by co-writing, producing and directing the live-action family film *Who Killed Nelson Nutmeg?* The film had its world premiere at the London Film Festival in 2015 and is now available on DVD/VOD. They now maintain Nelson Nutmeg Pictures Ltd alongside producer Jan Caston. This is the UK's only production company specialising in live-action family films.

http://nelsonnutmeg.com
http://ukscriptwriters.com
Twitter – @ukscriptwriters and @nelsonnutmeg

WEEK 1:
DEVELOPING THE IDEA AND STORY SHAPE

CORE CONCEPT

What's your core concept? What's the heart of your story involving the main character, their story objective and the conflict they face? A really good logline will have these elements in place.

For example: "A talented linguist is hired by the government to decode the cryptic language of aliens who have just arrived on Earth, and find out if they're friend or foe before the world takes its own defensive stand." (*Arrival*)

"A struggling actor wants to have a successful career, but when she falls in love with an aspiring jazz musician, their creative dreams could be the very thing that keeps them apart." (*La La Land*)

"A maverick New York cop comes to LA to save his marriage but gets isolated in his wife's office building just as ruthless terrorists take it over, and he faces a physical and emotional battle of wits if he's going to save the day." (*Die Hard*)

"A man suffering from short-term memory loss is on a desperate mission to find out who killed his wife, but he can never remember enough clues to build his evidence, and his condition makes him easy to manipulate." (*Memento*)

So, the template for a good logline is: "It's about (a character/characterisation) who (action/desire, goal) but (conflict, the thing that's getting in their way)." If you can distil your core concept into these elements, you'll have a great starting point to develop the shape of your story.

STORY SHAPE

The classic three-act structure form has five main story beats: inciting incident, end of act one, midpoint of act two, end of act two and final twist/denouement. Try to lay out these beats to create the skeleton structure of the script, and then you can put meat on its bones with the characters and plot.

Example: Arrival (SPOILERS!)

- <u>Inciting incident:</u> Amy Adams gets approached by Forest Whitaker to be the one to decode the aliens' language.

- <u>End of act one:</u> she accepts the role, and goes to the aliens' site.

- <u>Midpoint of act two:</u> the authorities get twitchy and prepare aggressive defensive tactics, plus the soldiers try to sabotage the alien craft.

- <u>End of act two:</u> the authorities begin to take action as the situation now seems doomed. Communication has failed.

- <u>Final twist/denouement:</u> Adams desperately tries to save the situation as she begins to realise what the aliens' real message means for the world, and for her personally.

You don't need to know the exact details of what happens in between your story beats, but laying them down in the development phase will help you see the basic potential of what you're going to write. It will also enable a quick start to the screenwriting process. We're not messing around here; we're not looking for perfection, we're looking to get a first draft done (perfection can come later). This first draft challenge very much follows the mantra: "**Don't get it right, get it written.**"

Play around with your logline and your story shape. Expand the storyline as much as you want (synopsis, outline, treatment). All of this is achievable in week one.

Better yet, if you can write the first five pages (it doesn't matter how bad you think they are), this will help you get a feel for the style and tone of the story, and you'll be properly underway.

3 TIPS

- Watch a wide variety of TV shows or films in your chosen genre – as much as you can from the classics, foreign films/TV and modern fare. This will help you fully appreciate and understand the genre, and give you ideas of what works and what doesn't.

- The logline approach forces you to think about the protagonist first. But you could start by thinking about your location, setting, theme or any other story element that comes to mind.

- If you find you've got a jumble of ideas and you're struggling to get to a defined logline, then use a mind map to help capture your thoughts in a more focused manner.

A mind map is a visual tool to brainstorm thoughts and ideas by connecting them to an initial concept or subject.

WEEK 2:
TREATMENTS

If you've already started writing script pages, great. It might be useful to establish page goals, i.e. two pages per day, ten pages per week, whatever you think you can realistically achieve. If you prefer some preparation and planning first, no problem. Focus on writing an outline or a treatment; and once you've got your outline ready, amend your page goals to fit your schedule.

OUTLINE OR TREATMENT

An **outline** is a broad summary of your story, typically anywhere between three and six pages long. A **treatment** is a more detailed summary of your story, and can be anything between six pages and however long you want. A treatment of between eight and ten pages usually indicates you've got enough story content.

If you want to be doubly sure you've got enough content, break down your story into sequences; twenty to twenty-five sequences should cover a feature. These sequences will give you an idea of how certain scenes might play and how your story will develop.

Example: Manchester by the Sea sequences

- Lee leads a pointless, isolated life in Boston;

he's a handyman but his clients don't understand or respect him.

- He gets an urgent family call and has to return to his hometown. At the hospital, he learns his brother has died and he visits his brother's body in the morgue. He ponders the family implications of his brother's death.

The difference between an outline and a treatment is in the level of detail. For example, if we were writing the outline for the classic film *Jaws*, we might start with something like:

Police Chief Brodie is called to the shark-bitten remains of a swimmer. His first impulse is to announce the closure of the town's popular beaches, drawing fierce opposition from local commercial interests.

But in the treatment, we might go into further visual detail:

A midnight beach bonfire. Drunken revellers enjoy the music and the banter. One particular girl flirts with a drunk surfer dude, and she encourages him towards the water for a skinny dip. The surfer dude struggles in his drunken state and falls asleep by the shore, his trousers around his ankles. The girl doesn't seem to mind, she's enjoying the refreshing swim in the moonlit-bathed water. But then someone, or rather something, does join her in the water.

In this example, the treatment is providing specific imagery and detail that we can embellish with the scene action and description. This is why a treatment is preferable. You could go the whole hog and do a scene-by-scene document where you describe what happens in every scene, right to the end, before you write the script. (These scene-by-scene documents are obligatory for TV, so if you're doing a TV script, prepare to do a scene-by-scene breakdown.)

Whatever prep you choose, don't waste time that could be spent moving forward with the story/script. We're not looking for perfection, we're looking for progress and getting a first draft done. Sometimes writing script pages without any treatment prep can be helpful in finding the style and tone you're after, whereas a treatment is an effective document to launch you confidently in the direction you're going to write.

But for now, in week two of this exercise, we want four things accomplished: a clear and focused logline, a basic shape to your story, an outline/treatment and at least five pages of script written.

3 TIPS

- In the first draft of your outline it's fine to put something like "chase goes here" or "big emotional scene here" if that helps you move forward. Try to get to the end rather than getting bogged down as you go.

- Some people prefer to create a beat sheet – a list of the key action (beats) in the story. This can be a useful tool, but you'll probably still need an outline or treatment at some point. See a beat sheet as a step along the way, rather than a replacement (usually).

- If you're having issues with the outline where the story could follow a couple (or more) plot developments/options, then write them all down and decide which one to choose once you're in the writing process.

A simple way of sticking to this writing schedule is to establish a weekly page count. One hundred pages of script over ten weeks is ten pages per week, which is two pages per day, writing only Monday-Friday.

WEEK 3: THE INCITING INCIDENT

As soon as you start writing a script, the first main story beat within the three-act structure template should quickly come into view.

The inciting incident is the moment when the introduction and set-up of the story changes, and the premise of the film begins. Typically, it revolves around the hero, and is sometimes referred to as "the call to adventure": the moment when the protagonist (or their world) is challenged and the story awaits their response. It happens early on in a script, usually around page ten or so.

A bad inciting incident will be a plot-point that seemingly has no connection with the hero or the set-up so far. A good inciting incident creates the central dramatic question of the film involving the protagonist and the story. The central dramatic question gives the film its narrative spine, i.e. what the story should be focused on (see week one) and what the audience expects to see.

For example: Forest Whitaker turns up in Amy Adams's office and asks her to help him decode the aliens' language. Central dramatic question: will Amy Adams successfully translate the aliens' language and save the world? (*Arrival*)

Casey Affleck gets a call to tell him that his brother has

died and he needs to come home and sort everything out. Central dramatic question: will Casey Affleck be able to sort out his family's situation and put the tragedy of his past to rest? (*Manchester by the Sea*)

Sadness accidentally loses Riley's core memories from the brain's command centre, much to Joy's dismay. Central dramatic question: will Joy and Sadness be able to save Riley's core memories? (*Inside Out*)

Luke discovers Princess Leia's message to Obi Wan, and she needs help. Central dramatic question: will Luke save Leia, join the rebels and help defeat the Empire? (*Star Wars – A New Hope*)

WHAT NEXT?

For most of us, inciting incidents aren't really a problem. They're a natural occurrence to kickstart the story proper and move things along. But what happens AFTER the inciting incident? After all, it's rare for the protagonist to act immediately on the inciting incident, even if they're interested in doing so. There's usually at least ten minutes of screen time where the protagonist will avoid the implications of the inciting incident.

So, there'll normally be another scene or sequence where the situation will either get worse, or the protagonist ruminates on what they should do, but eventually they will decide to respond to the inciting incident (make a decisive action to sort the problem out), which typically leads us to the end of act one:

- Amy Adams joins Forest Whitaker and the team to decode the aliens' language. (*Arrival*)

- Casey Affleck picks up his nephew and stays at the house, reluctantly and awkwardly assuming a role of responsibility. (*Manchester by the Sea*)

- Joy and Sadness head out into the unfamiliar territory of Riley's brain to rescue the core memories. (*Inside Out*)

- Luke joins up with Obi Wan to help stop the Empire. (*Star Wars – A New Hope*)

If you're just getting to the inciting incident, great, that's exciting. Keep going. Get another five or ten pages in the can. One page per day, two pages per day, whatever's achievable or feels right.

3 TIPS

- Are you going way past ten pages in your intro? Quite often, as writers, we feel that we need to spend time setting up the world first. This means the inciting incident happens too late. Try to ensure it's happening no later than page fifteen. You can introduce us to the world as the story and action develops.

* Does your inciting incident set up the central dramatic question of the film? Does it really shake the protagonist's world? Ask yourself, would everything carry on as normal for the hero if they ignored this call to adventure? If they could, then maybe you need to increase the dramatic conflict of your logline/core concept.

* The inciting incident could be personal; it doesn't have to involve things blowing up. In the film *Broken Flowers*, it's Bill Murray discovering he has a son he never knew about. So whilst this incident is personal, that doesn't mean it's small. It's big and life-changing to him.

66 *Remember, don't get it right, get it written.* 99

WEEK 4:
DEVELOPING
ACT ONE

Here's a basic breakdown of act one sequences:

* Set-up/Intro
* Inciting incident
* Reaction/Build-up
* End of act one decision

DIE HARD

* <u>Set-up/Intro:</u> John McClane's on his way to LA for Christmas. He's a maverick New York cop, he doesn't belong in the LA world. But it's his last chance to save his marriage as he heads to his wife's office Christmas party downtown. But at the office, he's not greeted with open arms and it's all quite awkward.

* <u>Inciting incident:</u> While John takes a moment by himself, terrorists take over the building.

* <u>Reaction/Build-up:</u> John doesn't know what to do. He doesn't even have his shoes on. He's on guard but outnumbered as he tries to get a handle on the situation.

* <u>End of act one decision:</u> Takagi gets killed – this is life and death – and John pulls the fire alarm, which will alert the authorities but also finally expose him to the terrorists. Now the battle commences.

It doesn't matter which genre you're writing, this basic guideline to your first act set-up should keep you focused on what needs to happen. If talk of three-act structure and similar lingo gets you down, then structure is essentially this: **making sure that what happens next, happens at the right time and place.**

You can open with a flashback or a flashforward, and employ a non-linear narrative if you want, as long as what happens next is happening at the right time and place for the story. You'll find that even non-linear narratives fit the first act set-up quite nicely.

MEMENTO

* Set-up/Intro: Leonard's obsessed with finding and killing the man who murdered his wife. But he suffers from short-term memory loss so he can't remember enough clues or what he's done previously. He kills Teddy, then wakes up in his hotel room, not sure what's happened. We realise we're experiencing the story in reverse form.

* Inciting incident: Teddy says he's there to help Leonard, but Leonard suspects Teddy is the one he's looking for. Has he finally found his guy?

- <u>Reaction/Build-up:</u> We learn more about Leonard's past. He speaks to someone on the phone, telling them about Sammy Jankis, a man with a similar condition to Leonard. He meets Natalie, who gives him evidence and clues.

- <u>End of act one decision:</u> He wakes up next to Natalie. Natalie's helping him because she says he helped her. Leonard begins to gather his fresh leads.

This act one approach will either help you with basic prep or provide a useful guide to your main story beats. Keep going, keep writing, and before you know it, we're into act two.

3 TIPS

- What if your film is an ensemble story? They can be tricky to write, but if you assign one of the characters as the protagonist, then that helps to keep the first act focused on their objective (which is often the group's objective too, e.g. Bill in *It*). This also applies to dual-protagonist stories (or buddy films) like *Lethal Weapon*.

- Feel your act one is mostly plot and not enough character? Don't worry too much as this sometimes can have unexpected benefits. An engaging plot allows the audience to see how the character(s) react under pressure, e.g. Indiana Jones in the opening sequence and first act of *Raiders of the Lost Ark*.

* Is convenient or random "stuff" just happening to move the story along? Try to ensure that the plot is being driven by the protagonist, especially if you want the audience to get behind their quest. Even The Dude in *The Big Lebowski* decided to get the money for his rug back. Nihilists, man!

WEEK 5:
RAISING THE
STAKES

We're getting into the thick of it now. We're moving into act two!

Act two is where your character and story develop significantly. In commercial terms (and this guide focuses on commercial fare), it's when the protagonist moves further away from their initial set-up in terms of what they have to do and who they do it with, and when things keep getting harder and harder. As a result, their character is tested, often both emotionally and physically.

For your first draft purposes, don't get distracted or stuck by what should or shouldn't happen in act two. Just follow your instincts and put down what you want to happen. However, it's important to note that things should be getting harder for the protagonist. In other words …

WE'RE RAISING THE STAKES.

WHAT'S AT STAKE FOR THE STORY?

This is identifying what the protagonist stands to lose if he doesn't take part in the story. Don't want to go to Mordor, Frodo? Then watch all of Hobbiton burn! Y'say you don't like your new partner, Riggs? Then prepare either to be kicked out of the force or to commit suicide, you loser! You just want to drive the spaceship home, Ripley? Then watch your colleagues die and prepare to be slaughtered yourself!

HOW DO WE RAISE THE STAKES?

Frodo in The Lord of the Rings

Well, the list is endless for the poor guy. The Black Riders, the Eye of Sauron, Christopher Lee, trolls, not to mention the Ring taking over his will and personality. Not an easy ride for the small fella, is it? But by fighting the stakes and overcoming the obstacles, his character goes on a thoroughly dramatic and emotional journey.

Martin Riggs in Lethal Weapon

Riggs doesn't care about his life or his new partner, but their investigation into a drug-smuggling operation makes them enemies to a group of former Vietnam War mercenaries. They want Riggs and Murtaugh dead, no matter what the cost.

Ripley in Alien

Keep John Hurt off the ship. Nope. Well, keep him in quarantine then. Sorry. Let's sort this out and go home. Not yet, sister. Watch John Hurt's stomach explode and spend the rest of the film in a dangerous game of alien and mouse while all your colleagues die, die, die.

OTHER GENRES

As you can see, the above examples are for action/adventure/thriller-type films where it's "easier" to raise the stakes. But for dramas, comedies and other genres, it may not appear as simple or clear-cut. Raising the stakes can be more subtle shifts in the characters' behaviour and simply putting things in their way that they'd rather not deal with.

In Sideways, what's at stake for Miles?

* He's waiting to hear whether his book is about to be published, and if it isn't, it'll be the sad reminder of how he's failed in life, not to mention his all-too-fresh divorce.

* The stakes are raised by Jack, Miles's irresponsible friend, who takes them on a more carefree wine tour than Miles would like, leading Miles to the verge of a nervous breakdown and an improbable romance when he has to face up to the failures in his life.

* His book doesn't get published. He wallows in self-pity. He doesn't act on Virginia Madsen's

obvious interest. But Jack makes everything worse for Miles at every stage.

A lot of your trailer moments will come from act two – it's where the bulk of the story's difficulties and developments lie. So keep going. Get your pages done at the very least, and that page count should be creeping towards the midpoint.

3 TIPS

- Avoid the "repeating stakes" syndrome. This is where you just throw more and more of the same thing at the protagonist. You could use a variety of intellectual, physical and emotional challenges for them to overcome.

- Is everything too easy in your draft? Maybe the stakes aren't linked to the character enough? If the hurdles don't hurt the protagonist, they aren't strong enough.

- If your stakes all feel a bit pointless and random, consider this – have you raised the stakes for your antagonist too?

"Don't make changes or stop to revise what you've written so far – just make a note of ideas and comments/critiques, and keep writing!"

WEEK 6:
LET'S TALK TV

If you're writing a TV script, then a similar style and approach to the ten-week guide is needed. First, work out the idea, or more specifically, the **core concept**.

CORE CONCEPT

What is the beating heart of the story?

Not just: "It's a crime drama about a mobster boss and his personal and professional difficulties", but more: "It's about a mobster boss who undergoes therapy to explore his personal and professional difficulties, but if this was ever found out by his peers, he'd be dead." (*The Sopranos*)

To help you discover your core concept, it's sometimes useful to brainstorm an "irony of character". We learned this from top TV legend Tony Jordan. Irony of character is when the idea and central character generates an amusing or intriguing irony, which then also suggests the kind of thing we'd expect to see every week.

Let's run this irony of character notion through a couple of successful shows.

In *Life on Mars*, a pedantic cop from the 21st century finds himself in the political incorrectness of 1970s police, and desperately wants to find a way back to his own time.

This presents a format (i.e. what the audience will expect to see every week) where John Simm's character tries to get back to his own time while cracking 1970s police cases with Gene Hunt and his team. The irony comes from his 21st-century politically correct approach as opposed to Gene Hunt's raucous non-PC habits.

Death in Paradise has the perfect irony of character (a stuffy English detective is sent to the relaxed Caribbean to solve murders), which makes it an easy pitch. Plus, the series has got the potential to run and run, regardless of the central cast.

Want to play the game? Think of your favourite show, or a hot new series, and see if it has an irony of character.

Homeland? A US marine returns home a hero after eight years of captivity in Iraq, but a driven CIA agent suspects he might now be a terrorist. There's a definite strong irony there which drives the series (is he? isn't he?), but for those who may argue that Claire Danes's character is the lead, then her character is a talented but highly unstable officer who's desperate to make up for previous mistakes. She's not just an elite CIA agent who can do no wrong.

Breaking Bad? A modest high school chemistry teacher gets diagnosed with cancer, so he starts making crystal meth to ensure his family have enough money after he dies. A *delicious* irony there, a neat hook, and one of the best dramas of the 21st century so far.

Of course, not all shows have an irony of character at their heart, but it's certainly a useful thing to consider when you're developing your core concept.

TV STORY SHAPE

Once you nail your core concept, you're ready to tackle the **story shape** for the pilot episode. In TV, this is pretty straightforward: a teaser and four acts.

The teaser is usually something dramatic or intriguing to pull the audience in. The first act develops the situation (the cops discover the murder) and ends on a story development/hook (a prime suspect comes into view). The second act twists the plot further (red herrings, new information) and ends on a bigger development/hook. The third act sees some professional and personal reaction, plus more twists and turns, and an "all is lost" moment or big dramatic development/hook. The fourth act wraps it up, with the story coming to a satisfying but unpredictable resolution.

3 TIPS

* Is your project a TV or film script? Now is the time to decide. Never sit on the fence and say "this could be a film or a TV series" as a feature film is a very different beast to a TV series.

* Do you know the slot? Where might your script sit in the TV schedule? It can seem premature to be thinking about that now. However, knowing what you're aiming for helps you to tailor your script for the time slot.

* Can your idea run and run? That is what broadcasters are seeking these days. Investing in a series is so risky and expensive that there needs to be the possible payoff that it can come back for season after season: "OK, we know what happens in episode two, but what happens in episode fifty-two?"

WEEK 7: THE MIDPOINT

The midpoint is a useful place in your script to raise the stakes and jeopardy beyond a point of no return; to ensure something happens to compel the protagonist further so they can't back down. Up until now, the hero has had the inciting incident (will they/won't they get involved in the story?) and the end of act one (they decide to actively solve the story problem).

As they advance into act two they may develop a romantic subplot, start to learn new things and make new friends/enemies. That's all gravy, but the story needs something else now.

If your hero could decide *"you know what, I'm done here, I'm going back to my life before the inciting incident came along"*, then that's a sign that there's insufficient stakes/jeopardy.

The midpoint stops this from happening, and pushes the protagonist further, raising the stakes/jeopardy.

* Emma Coats, when she worked at Pixar, likened the midpoint to the moment in a poker game where you bet all in. (Emma's also well known for "Pixar's 22 Rules of Storytelling" – check that out online.)

* Blake Snyder in his Save the Cat model describes the midpoint as the moment when everything is great or everything is awful: "The

main character either gets everything they think they want or doesn't think they want at all. But not everything we think we want is what we actually need."

* And Syd Field says the midpoint is where the protagonist seems furthest from fulfilling the dramatic need or objective.

We think making things a helluva lot worse for your hero at the midpoint is more effective than making them seemingly great. But as with any discussion about screenwriting craft, it's more useful to see working examples:

* The T. rex attack in *Jurassic Park* raises the stakes as things get MUCH worse now past this midpoint, increasing the pressure on the main characters.

* In Pixar's *Up*, the midpoint is when they get captured by dogs and brought to Christopher Plummer's villain character, which raises the stakes for Carl (the hero).

* In *Arrival*, the authorities get twitchy and prepare defensive tactics at the midpoint of the story while the soldiers try to sabotage the alien craft.

- In *Black Swan*, Lily's made the new star, much to Natalie Portman's character's annoyance. She's going to have to push herself if she's going to get what she (thinks she) wants.

- In *The Ring*, Naomi Watts's kid watches the videotape, so now she has to save her kid AND herself from the curse.

You get the gist. Midpoints can be tricky, but as long as the stakes are raised so there's no turning back for the hero, you're on the right track.

Remember, structure is essentially making sure that what happens next happens at the right time and the right place.

3 TIPS

- Is your midpoint exactly in the middle of the script? No? Don't worry, it doesn't have to be. But try not to let it come too near to the start or the end as the story will feel oddly paced.

- Does your midpoint lack an emotional punch? Then a few classic things to try are: a betrayal, a death of a colleague, a new arrival or a change of location.

- Does your midpoint feel a bit soggy or samey? It could be because the emotional or dramatic tone of the script is identical before and after your intended midpoint. Use the midpoint as a chance to shift the feeling of the story, to heighten the mood and drama.

WEEK 8: THE END OF ACT TWO

What in the name of all that's holy moly happens between the midpoint and the end of act two? The midpoint was the point of no return (something very bad turning the screw, or things backfiring badly, the stakes raised to the max). But what now?

Let's recap and breakdown some basic structural sequences:

ACT ONE

* Set-up/Intro
* Inciting incident
* Reaction/Build-up
* End of act one decision

ACT TWO

* Character interaction
* Plot development
* Midpoint
* ?
* ??
* ???
* End of act two

Getting to the end of act two can be confusing and difficult, but essentially you should be pushing the protagonist to their lowest ebb. We particularly like the

Pixar poker structure analogy by Emma Coats: "The end of act two is when you seemingly lose."

Blake Snyder's beat sheet recommends three key sequences to bring you from your midpoint to the end of act two: Bad Guys Close In, All Is Lost, Dark Night of the Soul. What we like about these sequences (which shouldn't be taken literally) is that they ensure suitable plot AND character development. For example, in *The Dark Knight Rises*, Bane takes control, he holds Gotham hostage, Batman's stuck at the bottom of that cave jail, his back broken, watching Gotham burn helplessly on TV.

It doesn't matter if you decide to embrace these specific screenwriting tips or structural methods; what matters is that your story advances in a way that's going to work for the genre and audience expectation.

Genre + tone = audience expectation.

Audiences already know structure, even if they're not consciously aware of it; and if you develop your story well, you're going to pile the drama and stakes on to the protagonist so that by the end of act two they're in a right slump, seemingly defeated.

But that exact downer moment of defeat is precisely what the pace and story needs to lift you towards the act three finale. (*The Dark Knight Rises*: Batman recovers and manages to escape the prison, heading back to Gotham to save the day). This structural approach is just common sense, really; a way to push audience buttons as well as doing your story justice.

Quick look at Mad Max: Fury Road (SPOILERS!)

- Inciting incident: Max becomes Nux's body bag.

- End of act one decision: Max decides he'll help Furiosa (note: to ensure his own survival).

- Midpoint: after the storm cloud, they move into wasteland territory, but Immortan Joe won't stop in his pursuit.

- The pregnant bride dies.

- They get stuck in the mud. Baddies close in, but Max manages to keep them at bay.

- They reach Furiosa's Green Place and they meet the Vuvalini.

- End of act two: Max is going to split up from the gang, and Furiosa is heartbroken about the truth of her Green Place.

- Act three: Max decides to go back, help Furiosa and the greater good, not just thinking of himself any more.

But ... what's that up ahead? What's in store for the remaining parts of this guide? Why, it's act three. A possible solution. It's a crazy idea but it just might work. Let's do it, let's give it our best to save the day!

3 TIPS

- Is it possible to write a script up to this point and not know how it ends? Yes, certainly. But remember in act one when your inciting incident set up the central dramatic question of the film? That question's going to be answered soon in act three, oh yes.

- Does your second part of act two lack focus and wander into a new story thread? Then backtrack a little, and refocus on the protagonist's main story objective/goal to see if you've lost sight of that.

- If your act two is starting to get confusing, then break it down by character. Write down how each character is feeling, what their goals are and what's stopping them. Sometimes another character starts to overshadow the plot and steal the limelight from the protagonist, and thus creates confusion.

WEEK 9: THE FINALE

Ho, ho, ho! Now we're in it. We're up to week nine of the ten-week writing challenge, which means – we've reached act three!

Here's what we've covered so far:

ACT ONE

* Set-up/Intro
* Inciting incident
* Reaction/Build-up
* End of act one decision

ACT TWO

* Character interaction
* Plot development
* Midpoint
* Stakes/Jeopardy to the max
* Worst case scenario
* End of act two

ACT THREE

* ?
* ??

So, act three, what the hell?

The legendary Billy Wilder once said that "If you have a

problem with the third act, the real problem is in the first act."

As cocky newbies we thought this was a neat quote, but we didn't necessarily agree with it. However, now that we've agonised over third acts on nearly all our scripts, we can confidently say that Wilder knew what he was talking about. Indeed, even the script we're working on for this whole exercise is running into the same problem, which is: the third act problems are first act problems.

Let's pick at it a little.

In act one, the inciting incident sets up the dramatic question of the film. Will Amy Adams successfully decode the aliens' language and help save the world? Will Joy and Sadness be able to work together to save Riley's core memories? Will Luke join the rebels and help defeat the Empire?

The inciting incident is thus setting up a basic audience expectation that the story needs to fulfil or pay off. In screenwriting land, they call this the **obligatory scene**. Sounds a bit dull, but it's the scene in act three that answers the core question of the film. If your act three doesn't have this obligatory scene already, that's one problem that can be fixed pretty pronto.

Great, the inciting incident/obligatory scene takes care

of one problem, but what about the rest?

Well, everything you set up in act one regarding your protagonist and their situation should probably be paid off or resolved in act three. The resolution should be causally and emotionally connected rather than the plot going off on indulgent tangents and giving the audience a vague sense of conclusion. It's about clarity of story purpose: what is your story ultimately about? What is it trying to say? And how is it saying it through the protagonist's experience and ultimate story outcome?

In *The Matrix*, the first act set-up introduces us to Neo, alone, feeling disconnected, frustrated, that there's something bigger and more important out there, and that he could be The One. The third act resolution is Neo finally embracing his destiny as The One, becoming a bigger part of a wider team who are dedicated to saving humanity, and he's in love with Trinity. All of his first act issues are resolved.

Act three is the exciting finale, so typically there'll be a face-off or confrontation of some sort, whether it be action adventure or domestic drama. But hopefully, everything else about the protagonist and their story issues will also be dealt with, and everyone leaves the cinema with a feeling of satisfaction (whether the ending is upbeat or the opposite). Act threes are usually quicker than act ones, with two or three sequences to get us to The End. No time messing around, just wrap up the story in a neat and satisfying manner. No need for long codas or examining the aftermath. Fade out – you're done, fella.

REMEMBER: DON'T GET IT RIGHT, GET IT WRITTEN.

It's a first draft. If it's rough as hell, it doesn't matter; you've got something to work on and revise.

3 TIPS

* Does your ending not feel satisfactory? That could be because you've wrapped up the plot, but not the emotional side of the story.

* Watch out for using a *deus ex machina* – an element that arrives at the end and magically resolves everything. If you do need to use such a device, then sowing the seeds of it earlier in the script can be done during your next draft.

* Does the ending feel too easy? Maybe the stakes aren't high enough. Or, more likely, we never really saw what was at stake or understood the effect of losing.

WEEK 10:
THEME

All stories have underlying ideas and subtexts which can be expressed in a basic form of theme:

* Greed
* Lust
* Death
* Love
* Power
* Corruption
* Revenge
* Family
* War
* And so on

Of course, having evidence of one or more of these ideas doesn't necessarily represent a theme in itself; how the story is resolved through character and plot reveals what you're saying about the theme (whether you're aware of it or not).

For example, say your story is about a man who cheats on his wife (suggesting a theme of lust/betrayal). This could be a thriller, horror, romcom, whatever you want. In the story, he gets away with his fling but finishes the affair, realising he's better off with his wife. However, his wife wants a divorce, feeling that their relationship isn't working any more. The man then tries to resume his relationship with the other woman, but is turned down and is left alone.

The theme could be saying that with love you can't have everything your own way (but there could be a hundred bloody corpses or a comic wedding for the finale, depending on your genre).

That's a simple example, but you get the idea. People may not pick up on the theme at all, depending on how the story is delivered, and will have just enjoyed the breakdown of the man's selfish behaviour. And that's perfectly fine. Maybe even the writer couldn't care less what the theme is, and is happily leaving it for others to come to their own conclusions.

When people mention theme, it conjures up pseudo-intellectual posturing about deeper meaning when there may be none in the first place. This is what makes theme a difficult subject. Generally, the audience doesn't want to be aware of it – not consciously anyway – and certainly not while they're watching the film.

YOUR APPROACH TO THEME

The usual comment about theme is that it should be invisible, and this is good advice to follow. By all means, layer your characters and story with your mind-blowing notions of whatever theme you're after, but don't bore the audience with dialogue lectures or insignificant scenes that support the theme (and do nothing for the story). Still, writing for theme works in a variety of ways. Let's take a look.

One: Don't worry about theme

Just get your first draft done, only then revising the story to add notions of theme and what you really want to say.

Two: Write with theme in mind

Many writers stick the theme, or even one word, over their computers to remind themselves that everything must feed into that idea and really get a hold of the resounding power of your story.

Three: Forget all about theme

Write what you like. If you feel confident that the story delivers what you want in terms of entertainment value but you don't have a clue what the theme is, don't worry. Someone else will come up with one for you, probably a critic (especially if the film is a hit).

Loads of hit films don't have themes, but that doesn't mean to say that they're hollow or without merit. The slimmest suggestion of a theme could be enough. It's a useful reference, and can certainly bolster your characters/story when you're fully aware of it, but don't trip yourself up trying to ensure that your script's got a thematic argument. That way madness (and boredom) lies.

3 TIPS:

* If you like the idea of using a theme, then the rewrite is the time to really get into it. Focus on the theme and riffing that through the script before making other changes.

* If you feel the theme isn't shining through as much as you would like, try having the protagonist and antagonist personify opposing elements of the theme.

* Having trouble articulating your theme? Maybe phrase it as a question that's going to be explored in the script. "Is it better to have loved and lost than never to have loved at all?"

A story's theme is dramatised through the protagonist's choices and behaviour, affecting how the story is resolved in a positive or negative manner.

CODA

Now that we've reached the end of this guide, did you actually get a first draft done, or just enjoy reading the tips? We've employed the ten-week writing schedule for our own spec scripts (last year we completed two new features and three new TV scripts, and got them up to a nice readable level) so we know it works.

However, your mileage may vary or you may have insights of your own on how to best use your writing time. If so, let us know and get in touch via our website ukscriptwriters.com, where there's also a host of free resources (our podcast, videos, blogs) and, of course, a handy link to where you can purchase our essential *The UK Scriptwriter's Survival Handbook*.

Now onto the rewrite!

Printed in Poland
by Amazon Fulfillment
Poland Sp. z o.o., Wrocław

53575191R00043